Traditional Italian Recipes

6

I Ristampa Maggio 2000
II Ristampa Maggio 2001
III Ristampa Maggio 2004

© copyright: 1998, maria pacini fazzi editore
via dell'angelo custode, 33
55100 lucca
tel. 0583/440188 - fax 0583/464656
e-mail: mpf@pacinifazzi.it
sito internet:
http://www.pacinifazzi.it

Proprietà letteraria riservata
Printed in Italy

ISBN 88-7246-315-7

A Taste of Tuscany

Sandra Lotti

maria pacini fazzi editore

This book is dedicated to my friends Tara Richmond and Liz Riley and to all the students of Toscana Saporita Cooking School.

A Taste of Tuscany

Everybody loves Tuscany for their own special reasons, among them art, architecture and the beauty of the landscape. But in the last few years Tuscany has become known as Italy's jewel for its cuisine, which, in a certain way, is related to art itself. This central region of the country, in fact, embodies all the features one thinks of when one thinks of Italy: beautiful Medieval and Renaissance cities; walled hill towns situated in the middle of nowhere; rolling countrysides with neverending olive groves and vineyards, that produce the best olive oil and wine in the world. The ancient Etruscans were epicures, as are modern Tuscans, and glorious meals are a big part of our lifestyle. Everybody knows the famous Ribollita Soup, and Fiorentina steak, but not everyone knows that the area's best-kept secret lies with its humblest ingredients: beans and bread. Saltless, rustic and yet the best partner to tuscan cured meats and pecorino senese cheese, bread is the main ingredient in Tuscan cuisine. What would Cacciucco, the most fa-

mous fish soup from Viareggio and Livorno, be without a slice of peasant style bread rubbed with garlic? Europeans consider this region the food center of Italy for its wines, cured meats and pecorino cheese.

But Tuscany has also had a terrible past and if what you see now glitters as gold, it once was as dull as iron because of the many wars and plagues, especially the one in 1527. The Maremma for example, where the Etruscans lived, was initially a severe and marshy land, but thanks to the Austrian family Lorena who, after Gian Gastone Medici's death in 1734, reclaimed the land, this southern valley is nowadays the agricultural engine of this region and a hunter's Eden. With this and other past problems resolved, Tuscany now offers the most varied landscape in Italy with its lakes, mountains, hills, valleys and sandy beaches. The best olive oil and wines come from this region as does the famous and rare white marble and the prized white truffle from San Miniato. The famous saying "If you go to the Maremma you are be rich in a day and you'll die in a year" is now discredited to the point where railroad conductors have stopped ordering people to shut the windows as trains cross the region. The scenery is breathtaking: Saturnia, the Etruscan Aurinia, obscured by the sulphurous vapours of its falls, appears like Dante's Inferno; Piti-

gliano, Sovana, Grosseto and many other hill towns dot this green happy land.

Driving through Tuscany today, you can lose yourself in the vision of the widespread fields of sunflowers brilliant under the blazing sun ubiquitous to this area. You can also feast your eyes on the limitless green of the wheat and the red clay color of the earth. Breathe more deeply than ever, ingesting the fresh and scented air, a rare quality that once breathed becomes part of you and forces you to come back. Join me in this adventurous cooking trip, take your time and be a little bit Tuscan. You will discover delicious recipes that tell the story of the great cooking of this magic countryside!

Sandra Lotti

Crostini con la beccaccia
Crostini with Woodcock

1 woodcock (a pheasant can be substituted), feathers removed, 1/2 cup extra virgin olive oil, 1 medium carrot, chopped, 1 celery stalk, chopped, 1 small red onion, finely chopped, 1 clove garlic, crushed, 1 bay leaf, 2 juniper berries, 2 cups basic beef broth, 3 tablespoons cognac, Salt and freshly ground black pepper, 16 tablespoons unsalted butter, at room temperature, 8 thin slices peasant style bread, cut into 4 sections each, toasted.

1. Heat the oil in a medium-size skillet, add the vegetables, the bay leaf and the juniper berries and sauté for 5 minutes over medium heat, stirring frequently.
2. Add the woodcock and brown on all sides. Pour the cognac over the woodcock and evaporate before adding the broth. Season with salt and pepper and cook, covered, for 45 minutes.
3. Debone the woodcock and puree the meat in a food processor along with the vegetables and cooking liquid.
4. Return the puree to the skillet; add the butter and cook over low heat, stirring. Set aside.
5. Toast both sides of the bread in an oven broiler. Spread the bread with the woodcock mixture. Serve hot.

Quarti fritti o panzerotti
Fried Bread Squares

In the past, when people used to make bread at home, fried panzerotti were the perfect accompaniment for cheese and boiled beans.

2 cups unbleached all purpose-flour, plus extra flour for kneading, 1/2 tablespoon wet yeast, 1/2 teaspoon salt, Extra-virgin olive oil, Olive oil for frying, Extra salt for dusting.

1. Dissolve the wet yeast in a cup of warm water.
2. Make a well with the flour and place the salt, oil and a half cup of the water/yeast mixture in the center. Using a fork, start mixing the ingredients, adding more water/yeast until all used up. With floured hands, knead the dough energetically until smooth and elastic.
3. Form a ball with the dough and place it in a large floured bowl, cover with a kitchen towel and let rise in a warm place for 2 hours.
4.When the dough has risen to double its size, place it on a large floured board and using a rolling pin roll it into a 1/2 inch thick sheet. Cut the sheet into 3 inch squares.
5. In a large skillet, heat 2 inches of olive oil.
6. Deep fry the squares until lightly golden on both sides.

7. Drain on paper towels for a few seconds. Sprinkle with salt. Serve hot.

Crostini dei butteri
Chicken Liver Crostini, Cowboy-Style

1/2 cup extra-virgin olive oil, 1 small white onion, finely chopped, 1 carrot, minced, 1 celery stalk, minced, 1 teaspoon chopped fresh rosemary, 3 leaves fresh sage, 2 cloves garlic, crushed, 1 pound chicken livers, diced, 2 ounces ground pork loin, diced, 1 red apple, peeled, cored and sliced, 1/2 cup dry red wine, Salt and freshly ground black pepper, 8 thin slices peasant style bread, toasted.

1. Heat the oil in a medium-size skillet and sauté the vegetables for 10 minutes over low heat, stirring frequently.
2. Add the remaining ingredients and cook, covered, for 45 minutes over low heat.
3. Place the mixture in a food processor and puree.
4. Spread the bread with the mixture. Serve hot.

Prosciutto e melone
Prosciutto with Cantaloupe

Tuscan prosciutto is more salted than the more widely known and more delicate Parma variety, and makes a perfect foil for sweet cantaloupes, with which it is often paired. Tuscan prosciutto also pairs well with fresh green or purple figs.

1 cantaloupe, seeded and cut into 8 wedges, 16 paper-thin slices Tuscan prosciutto.

1. Place 2 cantaloupe wedges on each plate.
2. Arrange 4 prosciutto slices alongside the cantaloupe or drape it over it. Serve immediately.

Olivata
Olive Presser's Paste

12 ounces oil-cured olives, pitted and finely diced, 1/2 cup extra-virgin olive oil, 1 clove garlic, 8 thin slices peasant style bread, toasted.

1. In a small terracotta bowl mix the olives with the oil until the mixture is well blended. Cover and set aside.
2. Toast the bread on both sides and rub each slice with the garlic.
3. Spread the bread with the olive mixture. Serve at room temperature.

Cecina
Oven Baked Chick Pea Cake

This delicious "invention" changes its name according to the province where it is made. In Lucca it is called "cecina", in Massa Carrara "calda calda" (hot hot), in Pisa it is simply called Torta, in La Spezia "Farinata". It can be served as an appetizer or a snack. Ground pepper is essential as a flavor enhancer and needless to say, the olive oil shoud be of the highest quality.

4 cups chick pea flour, 1 quart cold water, 5 tablespoons extra-virgin olive oil, Salt and freshly ground black pepper.

1. Pour the cold water into a large bowl. Whisk in the chick pea flour. Add salt and the olive oil.
2. Using a wooden spoon stir until smooth and well blended. The resulting mixture will be quite liquidy. Cover and let rest for one hour.
3. Preheat the oven to 375°F. Pour the mixture into a heavy-gauge, flat non-stick baking pan at least 1 inch deep and bake until a golden crust has formed. Serve hot, dusted with freshly ground black pepper.

Melanzane sott'olio
Marinated Eggplant

This dish is best when the eggplant has had enough time to completely soak in the marinade, for this reason start its preparation at least two days before.

1 large eggplant, approximately 2 lbs, peeled, 2 tablespoons salt, 8 cups water, 2 cups white wine vinegar, 2 1/2 cups extra-virgin olive oil, 2 tablespoons chopped fresh nepeta (or wild mint), 2 teaspoons fresh oregano, 4 large cloves of garlic, minced, Salt and freshly ground black pepper.

1. Dissolve the salt in a large bowl of water. Cut the eggplants crosswise into 3/4 inch thick slices. Place the slices in the salted water.
2. In a large pot combine 8 cups water and vinegar and bring to a boil. Drain the eggplant slices in a colander. Add slices to the water/vinegar mixture and cook for 3 minutes over medium heat. Using a slotted spoon transfer the eggplant slices to a dry kitchen towel, arranging in single layer. Cover with another towel and press lightly to absorb the liquid. Repeat for each batch, using dry towels. Drain for 1 hour.
3. Cut the drained eggplant slices in 3/4 inch cubes. Transfer to a large bowl.

4. In a small bowl mix together oil, herbs, pepper and garlic. Add salt to taste. Pour this mixture over the eggplant cubes, adding enough oil to cover.

5. Cover and let sit for at least 2 days in a cool place before serving.

Bruschetta

Everyone falls in love with its name and in the last few years it is on the menu of many italian restaurants in United States. The name Bruschetta, born in the Lazio, comes from the verb bruscato which means toasted on the grill. In Tuscany, Bruschetta is better known under the name Fettunta (oiled slice), simple to make and easy to understand. The classic bruschetta is a slice of toasted bread, rubbed with garlic, drizzled with newly pressed extra-virgin olive oil and sprinkled with salt. Depending on your choice of bread, salt may be added or omitted. In Tuscany, salt is used to compensate for the fact that the bread is all made without it, as has been done for centuries dating back to the Etruscans. For this and thousands of other good reasons, Tuscan bread pairs especially well with cheeses and cured meats, both of which are high in salt content.

1 loaf approximately 2 lbs peasant style Tuscan bread, sliced, 4 cloves garlic, peeled, Salt and freshly ground black pepper, Extra-virgin olive oil.

1. Cut the bread into 1/2 inch thick slices. Place on a grill or under a broiler and cook, turning once, until both sides are golden brown.

17

2. Rub each side with garlic.
3. Drizzle with extra-virgin olive oil. Season with salt and pepper and serve.

Panzanella

Rain, rain
Go away
Come again
Another day

8 slices peasant style bread, soaked in water and squeezed "dry", 4 ripe plum tomatoes, diced, 1 large red onion, diced, 1 cup red wine vinegar, Extra-virgin olive oil, Salt and freshly ground black pepper to taste.

Place all the ingredients in a large bowl and mix until well blended. Refrigerate for one hour. Serve cool.

Frittata di erbe selvatiche
Wild Herb Frittata

4 eggs, lightly beaten, 3 tablespoons extra-virgin olive oil, 1 medium white onion, finely chopped, 1 teaspoon chopped fresh thyme, 5 fresh basil leaves, 4 leaves fresh sage, 1 teaspoon chopped fresh rosemary, 1/2 teaspoon salt.

1. Place the eggs in a large bowl. Add the herbs and salt and whisk until thoroughly blended.
2. Heat the oil in a slope-sided, non-stick skillet. When the oil is hot enough to sizzle, pour in the chopped onion and stir frequently until lightly golden.
3. Add the egg/herb mixture and cook over medium heat until the bottom is slightly browned.
4. Slide the frittata onto a plate. Cover with another plate and turn over. Remove the covering plate and slide the frittata back into the skillet.*
5. Cook until the bottom is lightly browned.

* Note: instead of turning the frittata using the stove top method, you can also brown the frittata in a broiler.
Serves 4.

Zuppa alla frantoiana
Olive Presser-Style Soup

1 cup extra-virgin olive oil, 2 medium carrots, minced, 1 celery stalk, minced, 1 clove garlic, minced, 1 medium red onion, minced, 2 leeks, white part only, minced, 5 leaves fresh sage, 5 leaves swiss chard, stalks removed and roughly chopped, 1 medium head savoy cabbage, roughly chopped, 6 ounces canned italian plum tomatoes with liquid, squeezed until shredded, 4 new potatoes, peeled and diced, 2 celery stalks, diced, 2 medium carrots, diced, 3 small zucchini, diced, 1 medium fennel bulb, stalks and fronds removed, halved, cored and roughly chopped, 1 cup freshly-shelled peas, 2 ripe plum tomatoes, diced, 3 fresh basil leaves, 1 teaspoon fresh thyme, 1 pound dried borlotti beans, soaked overnight, drained and cooked with 2 cloves garlic and sage, Pinch nutmeg, Salt and freshly ground black pepper to taste.

1. Heat the oil in a large heavy-gauge pot over low heat. Add the minced carrot, celery, onion, garlic, leek, sage and cook, stirring frequently, until translucent, about 10 minutes.

2. Add the cabbage, swiss chard, peeled tomatoes and stir until well blended. Cook for 10 minutes.

3. Add 2 cups of cold water along with the remainder of the ingredients except for the salt, pepper and thyme. Increase the heat to medium and cook for 45 minutes.

4. Pass the beans and their liquid through a

food mill and add the mash to the soup pot. Cook for 1 hour.

5. Divide the bread among 6 bowls. Pour the soup over the bread and drizzle with extra-virgin olive oil.

Risotto ai funghi porcini
Rice with Porcini Mushrooms

1 medium white onion, minced, 2 cloves garlic, chopped, 10 tablespoons extra-virgin olive oil, 1 1/4 pound fresh porcini mushrooms, cleaned* and then sliced, 2 1/2 cups Carnaroli rice (Arborio can be substituted), 5 tablespoons dry white wine, 5 cups good quality beef broth, 1 tablespoon chopped fresh parsley, Salt and freshly ground black pepper, to taste, Freshly grated Parmigiano Reggiano.

1. Place the oil in a large and thick saucepan. Sauté the onion and garlic in the oil over medium heat, stirring constantly with a wooden spoon.
2. Add the mushrooms and cook for 5 minutes, stirring all the while. Add the rice and stir until it is completely blended.
3. Pour in the wine and cook until it has completely evaporated. Add the broth a little at a time, making sure that each addition is completely absorbed before adding more.
4. When the rice is in the last few minutes of cooking, stir in the parsley, salt and pepper.
5. Serve hot, dusted with grated Parmigiano Reggiano.

* To clean mushrooms, rub with a brush or a sponge. Never place mushrooms under running water as the caps act like a sponge and soak up too much liquid.

Gnocchi di semolino
Semolina Gnocchi

1 quart whole milk, 1 cup water, 11 tablespoons unsalted butter, cut into pats, 1 tablespoon salt, 1/2 pound semolina, Freshly grated Parmigiano Reggiano.

1. Preheat the oven to 350°. Pour the water and milk into a large pot, add salt and 8 tablespoons of the butter and bring to a gentle boil.
2. Pour in the semolina, whisking continuously to prevent lumps. Cook for 3 minutes or until the mixture is thick and soupy.
3. Pour onto a wet flat work surface and using a spatula to level the semolina to a half-inch thickness. Cut into 2 inch squares.
4. Place the squares in a non-stick baking pan. Dust with Parmigiano Reggiano. Dot with the remaining butter and bake for 10 minutes or until lighltly golden. Serve immediately.

Brodo di carne
Basic Meat Broth

Broth is the quintessential component of the
Tuscan Kitchen and the backdrop for a de-
lectable soup made with tortellini or pastina,
or even simply with croutons. This particu-
lar broth recipe can also be used when making risotto. The meat can be recycled into a
delicious casserole that also includes potatoes, herbs, extra-virgin olive oil, tomatoes
and onions.

2 carrots, peeled, 2 celery stalks, 1 medium red onion,
halved, 3 fresh basil leaves, 3 fresh parsley stalks, 2
very ripe plum tomatoes (or 2 whole canned tomatoes),
1 large meat bone, 1 leg chicken, 1 pound beef meat.

1. Place all the ingredients in a large soup
pot. Add 4 quarts water, cover and boil for 2
hours.
2. Strain broth and serve with croutons and
fresh grated Parmigiano Reggiano.

Intruglia alla Garfagnina
Bean and Sausage Soup, Garfagnana Style

1 pound fresh borlotti (cranberry beans), 1 large white onion, 3 fresh sage leaves, 2 cloves garlic, peeled, 1/2 cup extra- virgin olive oil, 1 ounce pork fatback, diced, 4 links pork sausage, removed from casing and crumbled, 2 medium carrots, diced, 2 celery stalks, diced, 2 cloves garlic, chopped, 2 large red onions, minced, 1 leek, white part only, chopped, 1 teaspoon chopped fresh thyme, 6 fresh sage leaves, 1 teaspoon dried dill, 1/8 teaspoon freshly grated nutmeg, 1 pound butternut squash, peeled, seeded and cut into chunks, 1 pound fresh kale, cut into thick strips, 3 cups polenta (coarse grind), Salt and freshly ground black pepper.

1. Place the beans, 3 leaves of the sage, the whole onion, 2 cloves of garlic and salt in a soup pot along with enough water to cover by 2 inches. Cover and cook for 1 hour. Add more water if necessary.
2. Place the oil in another soup pot and add the carrots, celery, minced onions, chopped garlic and leek, thyme, sage, dill, fatback and nutmeg and sauté over low heat for 10 minutes, stirring frequently.
3. Add the sausage and cook for another 5 minutes, continuing to stir.
4. Stir in the butternut squash, kale and a cup of the bean liquid. Cover and cook for 30 minutes adding 1 cup of hot water to maintain a liquid consistency. When the kale is

cooked, add salt and pepper, the beans and the remaining of the bean liquid. Bring to a boil.

5. Pour the polenta into the soup in a steady stream, stirring constantly with a wooden spoon. Add hot water to maintain a smooth consistency. Cook for 15 minutes.

6. Serve hot, drizzled with extra-virgin olive oil.

Cacciucco alla Viareggina
Fish Soup Viareggio Style

In Tuscany, there are three types of Cacciuc-co, each differing in ingredients and place of origin, according to the historic rivalries that existed among the Tuscan provinces. In the past, there was a huge debate on the origin of this creation. The Livornesi were said to have invented the dish. But it was subsequently stolen by Lorenzo Viani, the famous Viareggino painter, who "secretely imported" the recipe into Viareggio after having tasted it at a dinner party in Livorno in 1936. After that, the recipe became the property of every single Trattoria in Viareggio where Cacciucco was made using different types of fish to confuse the Livornesi. Since Viareggio in the old days was frequented by famous writers and intellectuals, the recipe was soon spread all over the world. Which is the best version? To be honest, I cannot say. But since I live in Viareggio and the famous painter Lorenzo Viani was from here... here is our own special recipe!

1/2 halibut, cut into chunks, 1 medium carrot, scraped, 1 celery stalk, 1 small white onion, 3 fresh basil leaves, 1 cup extra-virgin olive oil, 1 red chili, crushed, 5 cloves garlic, minced, 1 lb squid, eviscerated, washed and cut into strips, 2 calamari, eviscerated, washed and

sliced into rings, 1 small shallow water octopus, evis-
cerated, washed and cut into small pieces, 1 pound cray-
fish (or scampi), 1 pound blue mussels, 1 pound tender
white fish cut into chunks, 1/2 cup dry white wine, 1 cup
canned italian plum tomatoes with liquid, squeezed un-
til shredded, Salt and freshly ground black pepper, 2
tablespoons chopped fresh parsley, chopped, 16 slices
peasant style bread, toasted and rubbed with garlic.

1. Place the halibut, basil, carrot, celery and onion in a large pot and cover with water. Cover and cook for 30 minutes over low heat.
2. Heat the oil in a heavy-gauge skillet, add the garlic, the chili and sauté for 1 minute. Add the octopus, calamari and squid and cook over medium heat for 15 minutes, stirring frequently.
3. Add the crayfish, white fish and cook for 10 minutes, adding 3 or 4 tablespoons of hot broth as necessary to keep the ingredients from sticking to the pot.
4. Pour in the wine and cook until evaporated. Add the tomatoes and the remaining broth, cover and cook for 15 minutes.
5. Add the blue mussels and cook until opened. Sprinkle with parsley, add salt and pepper.
6. Serve hot on sliced bread, rubbed with garlic.

* Divide the bread among 4 bowls, cover with hot soup and serve.

Lasagnette al sugo
Lasagnette with Meat Sauce

The Besciamella Sauce

3 cups whole milk, 1 pound unsalted butter, 1 cup unbleached white flour, 1/2 teaspoon nutmeg, 1/2 teaspoon salt.

1. Bring the milk to a boil over medium heat. Whisk in the flour, the salt and the nutmeg, stirring continuously. Cook for 10 minutes or until thickened.
2. Add the butter and continue to stir until the sauce is smooth. Set aside.

The Basic Pasta

2 cups unbleached, all purpose flour, 2 cups semolina flour, 4 eggs, 1/2 teaspoon salt, 1 tablespoon extra-virgin olive oil, 2 tablespoons cold water.

1. Mix the semolina and flour together and pour the mixture onto a flat work surface. Make a well in the center.
2. Place the eggs, salt, water and oil into the well.
3. Using a fork, beat the eggs incorporating increasing amounts of the flour wall until a smooth dough has been created.
4. Knead with floured hands for 10 minutes.

5. Using a pasta machine roll the dough into thin sheets. Cut into squares. (Lasagnette)

The Meat sauce

1 cup extra-virgin olive oil, 2 medium carrots, minced, 2 celery stalks, minced, 1 medium red onion, minced, 3 fresh basil leaves, 1 teaspoon fresh thyme, 2 fresh sage leaves, 1 bay leaf, 1 clove garlic, minced, 2 pounds ground beef, 1 cup dry white wine, Salt and freshly ground black pepper to taste, 1/4 teaspoon freshly grated nutmeg, 1 large can Italian plum tomatoes with liquid, squeezed until shredded.

1. Heat the oil in a heavy-gauge pot. Sauté the vegetables and herbs for 10 minutes, stirring frequently.
2. Add the beef and cook over medium heat for 15 minutes, stirring frequently.
3. Pour in the wine and cook until evaporated.
4. Add the tomatoes and continue to cook for 20 minutes, covered.
5. Add salt, nutmeg and pepper, mix to blend and set aside.

Assembling lasagna

1. Bring the water to a boil, add the salt and 1 tablespoon olive oil to prevent lasagna from sticking.

2. Cook the lasagna for 3 minutes. Drain and place in a bowl of cold water.

3. In a roasting pan make layers of besciamella, meat sauce, lasagna and fresh grated Parmigiano, continuing to layer until all the ingredients have been used. Top with meat sauce, besciamella and grated parmigiano. Bake for 30 minutes at 350°F. Serve hot.

Tacconi alla Lucchese con Sugo di Lepre Falsa
Tacconi with Hare Sauce Lucchese Style

Tacconi in Lucchesia are a simple type of hand made pasta. The name Tacconi means "tacchi", meaning the soles of shoes and comes from the fact that they were made simply with water and flour. The resulting dough was so hard that the appropriate adjective became "dura come un tacco di scarpa" (as hard as a shoe sole!) Nowadays even the Lucchesi make their tacconi more lushly using fresh eggs and a few drops of their precious olive oil.

The Dough

1. 1 recipe basic pasta dough
2. Using a pasta machine or a rolling pin, roll the dough into thin sheets. Cut into small irregular squares. (Tacconi)

The Hare Sauce

1 medium carrot, diced, 1 stalk celery, diced, 1 medium red onion, diced, 2 fresh basil leaves, 1 teaspoon fresh thyme, 2 cloves garlic, crushed, 2 juniper berries, 3 whole cloves, peeled, 1 tablespoon chopped fresh sage, 1 teaspoon chopped fresh rosemary, 2 bay leaves, 1 cup extra-virgin olive oil, 1 farm-raised rabbit, cleaned and cut into small pieces, 6 ounces ground beef, 1 cup good red wine, 1 pound canned Italian plum tomatoes with liquid, squeezed until shredded, Salt and freshly ground black pepper, Freshly grated nutmeg, to taste.

1. Heat the oil in a large thick saucepan, add the carrot, celery, onion, garlic and sauté for 10 minutes, stirring frequently.
2. Add the sage, rosemary, thyme, whole cloves, basil, juniper berries and the bay leaf and cook for an additional 5 minutes.
3. Add the rabbit and cook for 20 minutes, stirring frequently. Using a slotted spoon remove the rabbit from the saucepan, debone and cut the meat into small chunks. Return to the saucepan.
4. Stir in the ground beef and cook for 5 minutes.
5. Pour in the wine, and cook until evaporated. Add the tomatoes, salt, pepper and nutmeg. Cover and cook for 30 minutes.

*Assembling the tacconi

Bring the water to a boil. Add a tablespoon salt. Cook the tacconi for 5 minutes and then drain. In a large bowl, make layers using tacconi, sauce and fresh grated parmigiano. Top the last layer with sauce and cheese. Serve immediately.

Delizie di Aldo
Aldo's Delicacies

Aldo Barcaroli is an extraordinary fish cook and this recipe is one of his favourite. Aldo is also the owner of the famous Pescheria La Sirena, in Viareggio.

The Dough

4 cups unbleached white flour, sifted, 4 eggs, well beaten, 1/2 teaspoon salt, 1 tbs extra-virgin olive oil, 1 tbs cold water.

The Filling

1 pound fresh sole fillets, 1/2 pound medium size shrimp, cleaned and deveined, 1 tablespoon chopped fesh parsley, 1 clove garlic, minced, 1/2 cup basic besciamella sauce (see recipe), Salt and freshly ground black pepper, Pinch of freshly grated nutmeg, 4 tablespoons dry white wine.

The Sauce

8 tablespoons unsalted butter, 1 pound fresh small shrimp, cleaned and deveined, 1 pound sole fillets, 5 tablespoons cognac, 1 cup heavy cream, 5 fresh basil leaves, 3 tablespoons pine nuts, Salt, Freshly ground black pepper.

The Dough

1. Heap the flour onto a flat work surface and

make a well in the center. Place all the ingredients in the well and blend until a ball has formed. Add more flour or water to maintain a smooth and elastic consistency, kneading continuously.

2. Using a floured rolling pin, (or a pasta machine) roll the dough into a thin sheet, place the filling in the center and fold. Cut each raviolo using a ravioli cutter or seal with a fork.

The Filling

1. Over a medium flame, bring the water to a boil; add the sole and the shrimp and cook for 10 minutes. Using a slotted spoon remove the fish, debone the halibut and flake with a fork. Mince the shrimp.

2. Heat the oil in a heavy skillet, sauté the garlic for 1 minute; add the shrimp and sole, salt, pepper, nutmeg and wine. Cook for 5 minutes, stirring frequently. Remove from heat and cool to room temperature. Stir in the besciamella and parsley.

The Sauce

1. Heat the butter in a heavy skillet on a very low heat, add the sole and cook for 5 minutes, add the shrimps and cook for another 5 minutes. Pour in the cognac and cook until evaporated.

2. Stir in the heavy cream, salt and pepper, pine nuts, basil and blend well until smooth. Set aside.

3. Cook the ravioli in a large pot of salted boiling water for 6 minutes. Drain and place in the skillet with the sauce. Sauté until well blended and serve immediately.

Infarinata di cavolo nero
Black Kale and Bean Soup

There are more than ten types of beans used in Tuscany. Among the reds are the Stregoni (warlocks), rossoni, rossi, scritti, dall'occhio, which are like kidney beans, and the cream of the crop, borlotti, which are the american equivalent to cranberry beans. The white quality includes piattelle (flat beans) corone (crowns) cannellini, fagiolane and the famous Sorana.

There is also a small black type called fascistini. Used fresh as shell beans, they generally require one hour of cooking time and can be cooked as part of the soup.

1 pound dried borlotti beans (or cranberry) soaked overnight and drained, 1 small red onion, 3 fresh sage leaves, 1 clove garlic, 1 cup extra-virgin olive oil, 2 medium carrots, diced, 2 celery stalks, diced, 2 leeks, white part only, chopped, 1 small white onion, chopped, 1 fennel bulb, stalks and fronds removed, halved, cored and then roughly chopped, 1 teaspoon fresh thyme, 3 canned Italian plum tomatoes, squeezed and shredded, 1 pound kale, stems removed, cleaned and shredded, 1 pound butternut squash, peeled and roughly chopped, 3 cups coarse-ground polenta, Salt and freshly ground black pepper to taste, Extra-virgin olive oil.

1. Place the beans in a soup pot along with salt, sage, onion, garlic and enough water to

cover by 2 inches. Cover and cook for one hour or until tender. When the beans are cooked, pass one half through a food mill along with the bean liquid. Set aside.

2. In another soup pot, place the olive oil and the diced carrot, celery, onion, leek, fennel and cook over low heat for 15 minutes, stirring frequently.

3. Add the kale, tomatoes and thyme, cover and cook for 10 minutes. Stir in one cup hot water.

4. Stir in the butternut squash, the whole beans and continue to cook for 10 minutes.

5. Add the pureed beans along with the liquid, salt and pepper and cook, covered, for 30 minutes.

6. Pour in the polenta and additional salt. Stir constantly using a wooden spoon. If necessary, add hot water to maintain a dense consistency. Cook for 20 minutes, always stirring.

7. Serve in individual plates drizzling with extra-virgin olive oil.

Farro con fagioli
Farro and Bean Soup

Barley-like in appearance and light brown in color, farro has recently been rediscovered by trendy Italians, who are as enamored of its taste and nutritional value as of the memory it evokes of a time long since past. Farro grows almost exclusively in the Garfagnana and its use has brought recognition to Tuscan cooking in general and specifically to that of this rugged mountainous region. Cooking farro requires patience: the patience required by a soaking period of 12 hours and the long time required to cook. As such, it brings to mind a way of life that once was standard throughout these mountain villages, a way of life that made it possible for the Garfagnana's women to spend all day making delicious soup and cakes for their husbands returning from the fields or the marble quarries. Farro was cultivated and consumed by the Assyrians and kernels were found in many of Egypt's acient pyramids. In Italy its use dates back to the Roman Empire. As the basis of their daily diet, farro enabled the Romans to become the powerful rulers they turned out to be. It was their primary food both in the form of kernels, which they boiled into a stew, and as ground flour, which they used to make a type of polenta called puls and the mola salsa, a type of porridge made with the toasted farro flour and salt. They also made a special cake called Labum that was offered to the gods. The precious kernels were also called "kernels of the power" because they were blessed by the goddess Demeter, wife of Pluto and goddess of earthly fertility. Farro is planted in October-November on graduated terraces that can be seen throughout the Garfagnana's hill towns. It likes water, but not standing in the water like rice, which is why it does so well in mountain settings. The grain itself is totally resistant to disease and therefore needs no fungicide or pesticide. It is harvested in June when the stalks are cut from the fields and allowed to dry for a few months before being beaten to remove the kernels. There are two types of farro: the gran farro, known botanically as Triticum Dicoccum; and the Triticum Spelta, also called farricello or spelt. The difference between the two types is that the Triticum Dicoccum needs a 12 hours soaking period while the Spelta can be cooked without soaking.

1 pound dried borlotti beans (or cranberry) soaked overnight, drained and then rinsed, 1 medium onion, 1/2 lb Pork rind or Prosciutto rind, 5 fresh sage leaves, 1 whole clove garlic, Salt, 6 ounces farro, soaked overnight, drained and rinsed, 1/2 cup extra-virgin olive oil,

1 medium carrot, diced, 1 celery stalk, diced, 1 medium red onion, diced, 2 cloves garlic, minced, 1 teaspoon chopped fresh rosemary, 4 fresh sage leaves, 1 fresh basil leaf, 5 canned Italian plum tomatoes, squeezed, shredded, with liquid reserved, Salt and freshly ground black pepper.

1. Place the beans in a soup pot along with the salt, pork rind, sage, onion, garlic and enough water to cover by 2 inches. Cover and cook for one hour or until tender. When the beans are cooked, remove the pork rind and pass the beans through a food mill along with the bean liquid and onion. Return to the pot.
2. Heat the oil in a skillet and sauté the carrot, onion, celery, rosemary, garlic, basil and sage for 8 minutes, stirring constantly. Add the tomatoes, 3 tablespoons hot water and continue to cook for 10 minutes. Pass the vegetable mixture through a food mill and add to the bean pot.
3. Bring to a boil and add the farro, cover and cook over low heat for 30 minutes. Add salt, pepper and hot water as necessary, to maintain a dense consistency. Serve hot.

Zuppa di ceci
Chickpea Soup

Dried chickpeas are among the hardest of the legumes and thus require 2 full days of soaking. They should be placed in a bowl with enough water to cover by 4 inches and let sit for 5 or 6 hours until the water has been absorbed. Additional water should then be added, and, after another 10 hours, that water should be changed. Many Garfagnini remove the skins from chickpeas after cooking and before eating because they say the skins are too tough to digest.

Just before serving this hearty soup, drizzle with extra-virgin olive oil and dust with freshly ground black pepper.

1 pound dried chickpeas, soaked overnight and drained, 2 large yellow onions, chopped, 3 medium carrots, scraped and diced, 3 celery stalks, minced, 1 cup chopped seeded tomatoes, 3 bacon slices, diced, 1 teaspoon chopped fresh rosemary, Salt and freshly ground black pepper, 1 cup extra-virgin olive oil, 16 thin slices peasant style bread, 3 cloves garlic, halved.

1. Place the chickpeas in a large heavy pot with enough water to cover by 3 inches. Cover and bring to a boil.
2. Add the carrots, celery, onions, rosemary, tomatoes and bacon. Cover and cook for 3 hours.

42

3. Heat the oil in a large skillet. Working in batches, add the bread slices and cook until golden brown, 1 minute per side. Drain the bread on paper towel. Rub both sides with garlic.

4. Using a blender, purée the soup until smooth. Add more hot water to maintain a smooth dense consistency. Return to the pot and season with salt and pepper.

5. Put the bread in individual bowls. Ladle soup over the bread and drizzle with extra-virgin olive oil. Serve hot.

Risotto con asparagi selvatici
Risotto with Wild Asparagus

1 large white onion, minced, 5 tablespoons extra-virgin olive oil, 1 pound wild asparagus, trimmed, woody ends discarded, 1 and 2/3 cups Carnaroli rice (Arborio can be substituted), 1/4 cup dry white wine, 4 cups basic beef broth, Salt to taste, 1 teaspoon unsalted butter, Freshly grated Parmigiano Reggiano.

1. Heat the oil in a deep heavy-gauge skillet. Sauté the onion over low heat for 5 minutes, stirring frequently. Add 3 tablespoons hot water and continue to cook until translucent.
2. Add the asparagus and cook over low heat for 5 minutes. Add 3 tablespoons broth and stir until well blended.
3. Add the rice and stir until well coated with the asparagus. Cook for 1 minute over high heat to toast it lightly.
4. Add the wine and cook until evaporated.
5. Slowly stir in the broth, adding additional broth as the rice absorbs it. Cook over low heat until the rice is tender (approximately 15 minutes).
6. Stir in the butter, salt, pepper and parmigiano and serve immediately.

Garganelli con verdure di stagione
Garganelli with Spring Vegetables

4 tablespoons extra-virgin olive oil, 1 medium carrot, scraped and diced, 1 celery stalk, diced, 1 clove garlic, crushed, 1 small red onion, chopped, 2 small zucchini, diced, 1/2 cup freshly shelled peas, 5 zucchini blossoms, cut into strips, 1 teaspoon chopped fresh thyme, 3 fresh basil leaves, 1 tablespoon chopped fresh parsley, 1 ripe tomato, diced, 2 tablespoons heavy cream, Salt and freshly ground black pepper to taste, Freshly grated Parmigiano Reggiano, 1 pound Fresh Garganelli (or other egg pasta).

1. Heat the oil in a deep heavy-gauge skillet. Sauté the vegetables over low heat for 10 minutes, stirring frequently.
2. Add the tomato, the zucchini blossoms and cook over low heat for 10 minutes. Add 2 tablespoons hot water and stir until well blended. Add the thyme, parsley, basil, salt and pepper.
3. Cook the garganelli in salted water with a little olive oil to prevent from sticking. Cook for 7 to 10 minutes or according to the package directions.
4. Sauté the pasta into the vegetable sauce, adding cream and parmigiano. Serve hot.

Tagliatelle a quattro colori con sugo di pesce
Four Color Noodles with Seafood Sauce

The Tagliatelle

4 eggs, 1/4 teaspoon salt, 2 tablespoons extra- virgin olive oil, 2 tablespoons cold water, 1/2 pound semolina, 1/2 pound unbleached, all purpose flour, 1 pureed peeled tomato, 1/2 pureed boiled swiss chard, 1 teaspoon squid ink.

1. Mix the semolina and flour in a large bowl. Heap onto a flat work surface, make a well and place the eggs, salt, water and oil in the center.
2.Using a fork, stir the ingredients, incorporating a little of the flour wall at a time, until a smooth elastic ball of dough has formed. Knead gently.
3. Cut the dough into 4 pieces, setting one piece aside. Give each remaining piece a color by adding the tomato, swiss chard and squid ink.
4. Knead each piece of dough until smooth. Using a floured rolling pin, (or a pasta machine) roll the dough into a thin sheet. Using the appropriate setting cut into thin tagliatelle.

The Sauce

3 cloves garlic, finely minced, 1/2 cup extra-virgin olive oil, 2 fresh squids, cleaned and cut into thin slices, 1 fresh calamari, cleaned and cut into thin slices, 4 fresh crayfish, 1/2 cup white dry wine, 6 canned Italian plum tomatoes squeezed until shredded, with liquid, 2 tablespoons chopped fresh parsley, Salt to taste.

1. Heat the oil in a large skillet and sauté the garlic for 1 minute.
2. Add the calamari and squid and cook for 10 minutes, stirring frequently.
3. Stir in the crayfish and sauté for another 5 minutes. Pour in the wine and cook until evaporated.
4. Add the tomatoes and mix until well blended. Cook for 6 minutes.
5. Season with salt and parsley.
6. In a large pot, bring the water to a boil, add salt and one tablespoon extra-virgin olive oil to prevent tagliatelle from sticking. Cook the fresh tagliatelle for 3 minutes. Drain and toss with the sauce. Serve immediately dusted with additional parsley.

Zucchini ripieni
Stuffed Zucchini

4 small zucchini, halved lenghtwise, 4 zucchini blossoms, rinsed and cut into strips, 1 small yellow onion, diced, 5 tablespoons extra-virgin olive oil, 2 eggs, lightly beaten, 1/2 cup freshly grated Parmigiano Reggiano, 1 teaspoon chopped fresh thyme, 1/2 teaspoon chopped fresh Italian flat-leaf parsley, 2 cloves garlic, minced, Salt and freshly ground black pepper to taste, 3 tablespoons unflavored grated bread crumbs, 3 tablespoons extra-virgin olive oil.

1. Preheat the oven to 350°. Using a paring knife or small spoon, hollow out the zucchini. Dice the zucchini flesh and place in a bowl.
2. Heat the oil in a heavy-gauge skillet and sauté the onion for 5 minutes, stirring frequently. Add 3 tablespoons hot water and cook until translucent. Set aside until cooled.
3. In a large bowl stir the eggs, the diced zucchini, blossoms, cheese, thyme, parsley, sautéed onion and garlic. Season with salt and pepper and mix until well blended.
4. Stuff the zucchini with the egg and cheese mixture and place, side by side, in an ovenproof baking pan. Sprinkle with bread crumbs and drizzle with oil.
5. Bake for 20 minutes. Serve hot or at room temperature.

Pollo arrosto alla contadina con patate
Roast Chicken, Farmers Style with Potatoes

The Chicken

1 free range chicken, 4 fresh sage leaves, 4 cloves garlic, Salt and pepper, Extra-virgin olive oil, 1/2 cup dry white wine.

The Potatoes

1 pound new potatoes, halved, 2 cloves garlic, sliced, 5 fresh sage leaves, 1 teaspoon fresh rosemary, Extra-virgin olive oil, Salt.

1. Preheat the oven to 350°F.
2. Make 4 small slits on the body of the chicken, one on each side of the breast and one where the legs join the breast. In each cut place a leaf of sage, a few slices of garlic, salt and pepper. Season the whole chicken with salt and pepper.
3. Place the chicken in a large roasting pan, rub with oil and cook for 40 minutes.
4. Pour the wine over the chicken and continue to cook for about 20 minutes.
5. Carve the chicken into serving pieces and arrange it on a platter surrounded with potatoes.

The Potatoes

1. Place the potato halves in a baking pan. Drizzle with extra- virgin olive oil. Sprinkle with rosemary and salt. Add the sage leaves and garlic.
2. Bake for 1 hour at 350°F turning once or twice during that period.

Pollo al vin santo
Chicken Cooked in Vin Santo

Vin Santo is an aged sweet wine produced in Tuscany which is usually served with Cantucci, typically Tuscan hard biscuits with whole almonds.

1/4 pound free range chicken, cut into individual pieces, 10 tablespoons extra-virgin olive oil, 2 large yellow onions, cut into 1/4 inch-thick slices, 4 cloves garlic, minced, 3/4 cup dry white wine, 1/4 cup Vin Santo, 1 tablespoon chopped fresh parsley, Salt and freshly ground black pepper.

1. Season the chicken with salt and pepper.
2. Heat the oil in a large heavy-gauge skillet, add the chicken pieces and brown on all sides (about 10 minutes in total). Using tongs, transfer chicken to a bowl. Cover and set aside.
3. Reduce the heat to medium-low. Add the onions and garlic and sauté until tender and lightly golden. Stir in the white wine and cook until evaporated.
4. Return both the chicken and its juices to the skillet. Cover and simmer over medium heat for 15 minutes.
5. Uncover and simmer for an additional 15 minutes, then pour in the Vin Santo and cook until evaporated. Dust with fresh parsley and serve immediately.

Patate rifatte
Potatoes "Done again"

When we say "rifatte" we usually mean cooked twice. But for this recipe the verb "cooked" is misused because the potatoes we use are raw. Only the meat is cooked. A culinary tradition dating back to the old days when poor people expended leftovers by adding new ingredients. In this case, raw potatoes.

1 cup extra-virgin olive oil, 1 large red onion, finely chopped, 2 cloves garlic, whole, 5 fresh sage leaves, 5 large potatoes, peeled and cut into small chunks, 5 fresh basil leaves, Salt and freshly ground black pepper, 5 canned Italian plum tomatoes, squeezed until shredded, 1 pound leftover beef or other meat, cut into chunks, 1 tablespoon chopped fresh parsley.

1. Heat the oil in a large heavy-gauge skillet and sauté the onion and garlic for 5 minutes, stirring frequently.
2. Add the sage and potatoes and cook for an additional 5 minutes.
3. Stir in the basil, salt, pepper and broth, cover and cook for another 5 minutes.
4. Add tomatoes and beef and continue to cook, covered for 10 minutes.
5. When the potatoes are tender, sprinkle with parsley, uncover and cook until thoroughly soft. Serve hot.

Porcini in umido con polenta
Sautéed Porcini Mushrooms with Polenta

The Porcini Mushrooms

1 cup extra-virgin olive oil, 2 cloves garlic, whole, 1 pound fresh porcini, scrubbed with a mushroom brush and sliced, 1 teaspoon fresh nepeta leaves (or wild mint), 1/2 cup canned tomatoes, squeezed and with liquid reserved, Salt and freshly ground black pepper.

The Polenta

2 quarts cold water, 2 tablespoons extra-virgin olive oil, 1 tablespoon salt, 1 lb. polenta, coarse ground.

1. Place the water in a large, heavy-gauge soup pot and bring to a boil over medium heat. Add the oil and salt.
2. Stir in the polenta, whisking continuously to prevent lumps and cook for 40 minutes over low heat. Stir frequently using a wooden spoon.
Meanwhile, prepare the mushrooms:
3. Place the oil in a non-stick skillet. Add the garlic and sautée for 1 minute, stir in the mushrooms, nepeta and cook for 5 minutes over low heat.
4. Add the tomatoes along with two tablespoons of the reserved liquid, salt and pepper and continue to cook for 10 minutes stirring frequently.

5. When the polenta comes away from the sides of the pot, remove from heat and distribute among individual bowls. Top with mushrooms and serve.

Carciofi alla nepitella e pancetta
Pan Fried Artichokes with Nepeta and Pancetta

8 artichockes, stems peeled, outer leaves and choke removed, Juice of 1 lemon, 10 tablespoons extra-virgin olive oil, 1 large white onion, diced, 2 cloves garlic, minced, 5 ounces pancetta (cured bacon), cut into small cubes, Salt, 3 tablepoons fresh nepeta leaves (or wild mint), 1/2 cup dry white wine (or lemon juice).

1. Cut the artichokes into eights and soak in lemon water to avoid darkening.
2. Heat the oil in a skillet and sauté the garlic, onion and pancetta over low heat for 10 minutes, stirring frequently.
3. Add the artichokes, salt, pepper and nepeta and cook for 10 minutes.
4. Pour in the wine (or lemon juice) and simmer for 10 minutes. Add 4 tablespoons hot water, cover and cook until tender, approximately 10 minutes. Serve hot.

Arrosto di maiale alla Fiorentina
Braised Pork Florentine

1 cup extra-virgin olive oil, 2 medium carrots, diced, 2 celery stalks, diced, 2 medium red onions, diced, 1 leek, white part only, cleaned and diced, 2 freh basil leaves, 1 bay leaf, 1 teaspoon fresh thyme, 1 pound pork loin, seasoned with salt and freshly ground black pepper, 10 tablespoons good quality white vinegar, 1 tablespoon balsamic vinegar.

1. Preheat the oven to 350°. Place the oil, pork, bay leaf,basil, thyme and vegetables in a baking pan and roast for 30 minutes.
2. Pour the vinegar over the pork and continue to cook for another 20 minutes.
2. Transfer the cooked pork to a cutting board and thinly slice. Keep warm.
3. Purée the vegetables along with the pan drippings in a food processor. Arrange the sliced pork on a serving platter and top with the vegetable puree. Serve immediately.

Sformato di fagiolini
Green Bean Mold

1 pound green beans, steamed until thoroughly softened and then diced, 2 cups basic besciamella sauce, 8 ounces mortadella (italian bologna) diced, 4 ounces freshly grated Parmigiano Reggiano, 2 large eggs, Salt and freshly ground black pepper, 1 cup unflavored breadcrumbs, 4 tablespoons butter, softened at room temperature.

1. Preheat the oven to 350°.
2. Place all the ingredients in the bowl of a food processor and puree.
3. Grease a round 10-inch pan with butter and spread with breadcrumbs.
4. Pour in the puree, level with a spatula, dust with breadcrumbs and bake for 30 minutes.
5. Slice the bean mold and serve hot.

Cinghiale alla cacciatora con polenta
Wild Boar, Hunters Style

The Marinade

4 cups dry red wine, 1 cup red wine vinegar, 2 medium carrots, diced, 1 tablespoon thyme, 1 medium red onion, sliced, 1 tablespoon fresh parsley leaves, 5 bay leaves, 10 juniper berries.

The Boar

1 cup extra-virgin olive oil, 3 cloves garlic, crushed, 1

tablespoon fresh rosemary, 3 pounds loin of boar, 4 tablespoons unbleached all purpose flour, 1 cup canned Italian plum tomatoes, liquid reserved, 1 cup oil-cured olives, 1 cup dry white wine, Salt and freshly ground black pepper.

1. Rinse the meat in cold water and dry on paper towels. Blend together all the ingredients for the marinade, pour over meat and let sit for at least 24 hours, turning four times to make sure the flavor is absorbed.

2. Remove the meat from the marinade and drain, reserving one cup of the liquid.

3. Heat the oil in a heavy-gauge pot, add the garlic and rosemary and sauté for 1 minute. Add the meat and sauté until browned on all sides.

4. Dust the meat with the flour and continue to cook until the sauce is somewhat thickened.

5. Pour in the reserved marinade and cook until evaporated, stirring to blend all the ingredients.

6. Add the tomatoes and half cup of hot water, cover and continue to cook for 20 minutes.

7. In a separate saucepan, cover and cook the olives in the white wine for 2 minutes over medium heat. Transfer the cooked olives to the pot with the meat and seasonings.

8. Cook for 2 hours, adding a tablespoon or two of hot water when necessary to prevent sticking.

9. Serve with hot polenta.

Frittelle di baccalà (Cod)
Baccalà Fritters

In olden times, Catholics were required to abstain from eating meat on Friday. In many houses, this tradition continues with vegetables, cheese or fish substituting as that day's entree. The following is a typical Friday recipe. For this preparation, the baccalà must be soaked for at leat two days to soften its flesh and remove the salt.

1 pound cod (soaked for 48 hours in cold water. The water should be changed 5 or 6 times during that period), 1 cup unbleached flour, Milk, Olive oil for frying, Salt.

1. Rinse the baccalà and place it in a medium sized pot with enough water to cover it. Bring to a boil and cook for 10 minutes.
2. Drain the baccalà and flake the flesh using a fork. Remove the bones.
3. Place the baccalà flakes into a bowl. Add the flour and milk and, using a wooden spoon, blend until a creamy mixture has formed. The mixture should be not too hard nor too liquid.
4. Heat the oil in a large skillet.* Using a spoon pour the mixture into the frying oil. When each fritter is golden on all sides, re-

move and drain on paper towels. Sprinkle with salt and serve hot.

* Oil is ready for frying when a small piece of bread immersed in the oil sizzles around the edges.

Cima ripiena alla Lucchese
Stuffed Veal Breast Lucchese-Style

In Tuscany, we love to stuff everything: from vegetables to fish, from turkey to eggs. The translation for cima is summit. Why this cut of meat is called cima remains a mistery for me!

The Cima

1/4 lb boned veal breast, 1/2 lb veal loin, ground, 4 ounces Mortadella (italian bologna) chopped, Freshly ground black pepper, 1 tablespoon chopped fresh parsley, 5 eggs, lightly beaten, 1 cup freshly grated Parmigiano Reggiano, 1 teaspoon fresh thyme, 2 cloves garlic, minced.

The Broth

2 small carrots, 1 celery stalk, 1 small red onion, 5 basil leaves, Veal bones (taken from the knee), Salt.

1. Place the ground veal, mortadella, Parmi-

giano, eggs, thyme, parsley and garlic in a large bowl and mix until well blended. Season with salt and ground pepper and mix until well blended.

2. Spoon the filling into the veal pocket, and sew the end shut with a kitchen thread. Wrap the breast in a layer of cheese cloth and twist the ends tightly to seal.

3. Place all the ingredients for the broth in a large pot, add the gauze-wrapped breast and add enough cold water to cover. Bring to a boil over high heat. Reduce heat to medium and simmer for 2 hours, skimming away the foam as it rises. Add salt.

4. Remove the cima from the broth, place on a large platter and cut into 1/2 inch slices.

5. Serve hot.

Cenci fritti
Fried Clothes

These fried sweets take their name from Prato, one of the ten Tuscan provinces where fabrics are produced and also recycled. "We can do everything you want with your used clothes...even fry them!" the Pratesi used to say, jokingly. A year-round delight, these sweets are especially sought during Carnival when they appear in every shape: pinwheels; knots; stripes; diamonds and even squares. These cenci are among the oldest desserts in history. The ancient Roman street vendors used to make them during festivals dedicated to the god Bacchus in 500 B.C. The same recipe has different names according to the region where it is made: Chiacchere in Milan; Galani in Venice; Frappe in Rome.

2 1/2 cups unbleached, all purpose flour, sifted, 1/3 cup sugar, 2 eggs plus 1 egg yolk, 1 pinch salt, 2 tablespoons rum or grappa, 1 tablespoon unsalted butter, at room temperature, 1 tablespoon grated lemon peel, 1/2 teaspoon baking powder, Oil for frying, Confectioners' sugar.

1. Heap the flour onto a flat work surface and make a well in the center, add all the ingredients to the well.
2. Using a fork, mix the ingredients incorpo-

rating the flour a little at a time until a smooth dough has formed.

3. With floured hands knead gently for 5 minutes. Form the dough into a ball, wrap in plastic and refrigerate for one hour.

4. On a lightly floured surface and using a rolling pin, roll the cooled dough into 1 inch thick sheets.

5. Cut the sheet into stripes or squares.

6. In a large skillet, heat the oil over high heat until it sizzles. Fry the dough on both sides, then drain on a paper towel and cool to room temperature. Dust with confectioners' sugar and serve.

Gelato agli amaretti
Amaretto Gelato

4 egg yolks, 1/2 cup sugar, 1 teaspoon vanilla powder, 1 teaspoon lemon zest, grated, 2 cups whole milk, 1 cup amaretti cookies, crumbled.

1. Whisk the yolks and sugar in a large bowl until fluffy. Stir in the vanilla and lemon zest.

2. Whisk in the whole milk and the finely crumbled amaretti.

3. Process the mixture in an ice cream maker according to directions. Serve with Amaretto liqueur.

Dolce di Natale
Christmas Eve Cake

1/2 cup raisins, 13 dried figs, stemmed and chopped, 6 tablespoons grappa, 1 cup walnuts, lightly toasted, coarsley chopped, 2/3 cup pine nuts, 1 tablespoon grated orange peel, 3 2/3 cups all purpose flour, 2 teaspoons baking powder, 1/4 teaspoon salt, 1/2 cup unsalted butter, at room temperature, 3/4 cup sugar, 3 eggs, 1/4 cup whole milk.

1. Preheat the oven to 375°F. In a bowl cover the raisins with hot water and soak for 10 minutes. Drain and place in a medium bowl along with the figs, walnuts, pine nuts, orange peel and grappa. Cover and set aside for 30 minutes.
2. In another large bowl sift together flour, baking powder and salt.
3. In a medium bowl beat the butter and sugar until fluffy and creamy. Beat in eggs, one at a time. Add half of the dry ingredients into butter mixture, stir. Mix in milk and the remaining dry ingredients. Fold in nut mixture.
4. Transfer the batter to a 10-inch round pan. Bake until tester inserted into center comes out clean, about one hour. Remove from pan and cool on a rack. Serve at room temperature.

Cantucci all'arancia e mandorle
Almond and Orange Cantucci

3 cups all purpose flour, 4 teaspoons baking powder, 1 cup sugar, 7 tablespoons unsalted butter, at room temperature, 3 large eggs, 3/4 cup chopped blanched almonds, 1 tablespoon orange zest, finely grated, 1 egg yolk, well beaten.

1. Preheat the oven to 350°. Line 3 baking sheets with lightly-floured waxed paper.
2. Sift the flour and baking powder into a medium bowl.
3. Beat the sugar and butter in a large bowl until blended. Add the eggs, one at a time, beating until fluffy.
4. Mix in the orange zest and almonds. Add the flour mixture and beat until well blended.
5. Divide the dough into 3 sections and shape each into a long, slightly flat oval. Place the ovals on the baking sheets and bake for 15 minutes.
6. Cut the cooked dough diagonally into 1/2 inch thick slices. Return to the baking pan and bake until lightly golden.
7. Serve at room temperature with Vin Santo.

Tiramisù
Mascarpone Tart

For this recipe we usually use Pavesini biscuits, but you can also use Lady fingers or sponge cake.

4 eggs, separated, 8 tablespoons sugar, 1 pound mascarpone, 1/8 teaspoon salt, 1/2 pound sponge cake (or 40 Lady fingers or Pavesini), 1 cup brewed espresso coffee, 3 tablespoons cocoa powder.

1. Beat the egg yolks with the sugar until smooth and fluffy. Add the mascarpone and beat until well blended.
2. Using a whisk, beat the egg whites and salt until stiff peaks have formed. Fold the egg whites gently into the mascarpone/egg mixture. Set aside.
3. Dip the sponge cake in the brewed coffee and place on a plate to drain.
4. Assemble the tiramisu using the drained sponge cake as the bottom layer. Spread with mascarpone and continue layering with cake and cream until all ingredients have used. The top layer must be cream.
5. Sprinkle with cocoa powder and refrigerate for two hours before serving.

Crostata di ricotta
Fresh Sheep's Milk Ricotta and Pine Nut Cake

The Crust

2 cups plus 2 tablespoons unbleached, all purpose flour, 1 teaspoon baking powder, 1/4 teaspoon salt, 1/2 cup plus 2 tablespoons unsalted butter, at room temperature, 3/4 cup sugar, 2 eggs, 1 teaspoon vanilla extract.

The Filling

12 ounces fresh ricotta, 1/2 cup sugar, 2 eggs, 2 egg yolks, 3 tablespoons pine nuts, 3/4 cup raisins soaked in rum, 1 tablespoon grated lemon zest, 3 tablespoons chocolate chips.

The Crust

1. Place the flour, baking powder and salt in a medium bowl.
2. In another small bowl, beat the butter and sugar using an electric mixer until fluffy and smooth. Beat in eggs and vanilla.
3. Add the flour, baking powder and salt mixture and beat until all ingredients are well blended into a smooth and elastic dough.
4. Turn the dough out onto floured surface and divide in two halves.
5. Using a floured rolling pin, flatten each

half into disk, wrap in plastic and refrigerate for 1 hour.

The Filling

1. Preheat the oven to 375° F. Butter a 9 inch-diameter glass pie dish and using a spatula, press the ricotta through a strainer into a large bowl. Stir in the sugar, eggs, egg yolks, raisins, pine nuts, chocolate chips, rum and lemon zest.
2. Roll out each dough disk on a lightly floured surface. Transfer one disk to a 9 inch-diameter buttered glass pie dish.
4. Transfer the filling to crust-lined dish.
5. Cover with the second disk of dough, trimming overhang to 1/2 inch. Fold edges under and pinch together to seal.
6. Using a fork, pierce top crust in several places.
7. Using foil, cover the top crust to prevent from browning too quickly.
8. Bake the pie for 40 minutes or until the top crust is lighltly golden.
9. Cool on a rack. Serve at room temperature.

Ricciarelli di Siena
Siena's Almond Paste

2 cups almonds, 1/2 cup pine nuts, 2 cups sugar, 1/2 cup confectioners' sugar, 1 teaspoon grated orange peel, 3 egg whites, beaten into stiff peaks, 20 wafers.

1. Using a mortar and a wooden pestle, finely crush the almonds and pine nuts.
2. Place the mixture in a large bowl, add sugar, confectioner's sugar, orange peel and stir until well blended.
3. Gently fold the egg whites into the nut mixture.
4. Using a wooden spoon pour the mixture on individual wafers. Let rest for 6 hours.
5. Preheat the oven to 350°F. Bake the ricciarelli for 15 minutes.
6. Remove from the oven and cool on a rack. Serve at room temperature dusted with confectioners' sugar.

Castagnaccio
Traditional Chestnut Flour Cake

This is the most common winter cake in Tuscany. Its name varies according to the province that makes it: for example in Massa Carrara it is called "pattona" and in Versilia "Torta di neccio". When chestnut time arrives one can find this cake everywhere: from the most famous restaurants to the humblest homes.

4 cups chestnut flour, 1 cup water, 1 tablespoon grated orange rind, 4 tablespoons pine nuts, 1 teaspoon fresh rosemary, 2 tablespoons extra-virgin olive oil plus 1 tablespoon for greasing, 2 cups fresh sheep's milk ricotta.

1. Place the flour in a large bowl. Using a wooden spoon stir in cold water, a tablespoon at a time, until the resulting dough is creamy and smooth. If the consistency is hard, add more water.
2. Add the pine nuts, rosemary, oil and the grated orange rind. Mix until well blended. Preheat the oven to 350°F.
3. Pour the olive oil in a 9 inch-diameter round baking pan. Pour in the chestnut mixture and drizzle with few drops of olive oil.
4. Bake the castagnaccio for 45 minutes or until a crispy crust has formed. Remove from

pan and cool on a rack. Serve at room temperature with ricotta.

Torta della nonna, di Lisa Contini Bonacossi
Lisa Contini Bonacossi's Grandmother's Cake

Lisa Contini Bonacossi is a very special type of grandmother, a little bit different from the "grannies" we are used to. Even if she insists on saying that she has nothing more than other grandmothers, I disagree with her. First she is a learned chemist whose expertise made Carmignano wine so famous; second she is Ugo Contini Bonacossi's wife, and for this reason, a Countess. Neverthless, although she has a personal chef who prepares delicious cakes of his own, she herself chooses to make the following Ricotta and Cream cake for her 14 beloved grandchildren. Contessa Bonacossi was very proud to give me this recipe that is part of her family and of Capezzana Estate. When her grandchildren visit her, she told me, she puts aside everything to dedicate all her time to them. The best she can do is doing what all grannies usually do: making wonderful cakes for their grandchildren.

The Crust

2 cups plus 2 tablespoons unbleached flour, 1 teaspoon baking powder, 1/4 teaspoon salt, 1/2 cup plus 2 tablespoons unsalted butter, at room temperature, 3/4 cup sugar, 2 eggs, 1 teaspoon vanilla extract.

The Filling

3 egg yolks, 4 tablespoons sugar, 1 tablespoon grated lemon peel, 1 tablespoon unbleached flour, 1 teaspoon confectioners' sugar, 2 cups warm milk, 1 cup fresh ricotta, 2 tablespoons lightly toasted almonds, ground, Confectioners' sugar.

The Crust

1. Place the flour, baking powder and salt in a medium bowl and stir until well blended.
2. In another small bowl, using an electric mixer, beat the butter and sugar until fluffy and smooth.
3. Beat in the eggs and vanilla. Add the flour, baking powder and salt mixture and beat until well blended into a smooth dough.
4. Turn the dough out onto floured surface and divide in two halves.
5. Flatten each half into disk, wrap in plastic and refrigerate for 1 hour.

The Filling

1. Preheat the oven to 375° F. Butter a 9 inch-diameter glass pie dish.
2. In a medium bowl beat egg yolks and sugar until smooth and fluffy. Stir in grated lemon peel, flour and confectioners' sugar. Stir until well blended. Pour in the warm milk, blend. Transfer the mixture to a stainless steel pot. Cook this cream over low heat using a wooden spoon and stirring constantly. When the cream consistency is thick enough, remove from heat and allow it to cool.
3. Using a spatula, press ricotta through a strainer into a large bowl. Stir in egg cream and ground almonds until well blended
4. Roll out each dough disk on a lighltly floured surface. Transfer one disk to a 9 inch-diameter buttered glass pie dish.
5. Transfer the filling to crust-lined dish.
6. Cover with the second disk of dough, trimming overhang to 1/2 inch. Fold edges under and pinch together to seal.
7. Using a fork, pierce top crust in several places.
8. Using foil, cover the top crust to prevent from browning too quickly.
9. Bake the pie for 45 minutes or until the top crust is lighltly golden.
10. Cool on a rack. Serve at room temperature dusted with confectioners' sugar.

Torta di riso coi becchi
Easter Rice and Chocolate Cake

Becchi in Tuscany means "scalloped edges"
a word reminiscent of the towers of ancient
medieval castles.

For the dough

2 cups unbleached flour, 1/2 cup sugar, 1/2 cup unsalted
butter, softened to room temperature, 1 teaspoon vanilla
powder, A pinch of sea salt, 2 eggs, 1 teaspoon grated
lemon peel, 1/2 teaspoon baking powder.

For the filling

1 cup Arborio rice cooked in 1 quart milk along with
1 lemon rind, until softened, 8 ounces bitter chocolate,
1/2 cup sweet cocoa powder, 1 cup sugar, 2 eggs plus
1 egg yolk, 1/2 cup pine nuts, 1/2 cup candied fruit, 1/
2 cup golden raisins, soaked in rum for 2 hours and
then drained, 6 tablespoons Amaretto di Saronno li-
queur, 10 tablespoons Maraschino liqueur, 5 table-
spoons Sassolino (Anisette), Butter for greasing the
cake pan.

The Crust

1. Place the flour, baking powder and salt in a medium bowl and stir until well blended.
2. In another small bowl, using an electric mixer, beat the butter and sugar until fluffy and smooth.

3. Beat in the eggs, lemon peel and vanilla. Add the flour, baking powder and salt mixture and beat until well blended into a smooth dough.

4. Turn the dough out onto floured surface and with floured hands knead gently for 5 minutes. Form the dough into a ball, wrap in plastic and refrigerate for one hour.

The Filling

1. Preheat the oven to 350°F. Butter a 9 – inch cake pan whose sides are at least 3 iches high.

2. In a large bowl place the warm rice, chocolate and cocoa powder and using a wooden spoon stir until all the ingredients are thoroughly blended.

3. Stir in the sugar, pine nuts, raisins with rum, candied fruit and liqueurs.

3. Add the eggs, one at a time and mix well.

4. Bring the dough to room temperature. On a lightly floured surface and using a rolling pin, roll out the dough to a diameter of 12 inches and 1/8 inch thick. Reserve the handful for the topping. Arrange the dough in the buttered cake pan; overlap the edges. Pour the rice/chocolate mixture into the pan; roll the edges and flatten between thumb and forefinger to form a shaped edge standing at least 1 inch higher than the edge of the pan.

Using a knife, cut the edge into a pattern resembling a series of small towers. Roll out the reserved dough. Cut into 1 inch wide strips. Arrange on top of the cake in a lattice pattern.

5. Bake for 45 minutes. Remove from pan and cool on a rack. Serve at room temperature.

Indice

Traditional Italian Recipes
PUBLISHED PRICE
EURO 4,13

finito di stampare
nel mese di maggio 2004
dalla tipografia menegazzo/lucca
per conto di mp maria pacini fazzi editore